cannibal in the mirror

ALSO BY PAUL FLEISCHMAN

Picture Books
Weslandia
Time Train
Shadow Play
Rondo in C
The Birthday Tree

Novels
Whirligig
Seedfolks
Bull Run
The Borning Room
Saturnalia
Rear-View Mirrors
Path of the Pale Horse
The Half-A-Moon Inn
A Fate Totally Worse Than Death

Short Stories
Coming-and-Going Men:
Four Tales
Graven Images:
Three Stories

Poetry
Joyful Noise: Poems for
Two Voices
I Am Phoenix: Poems for
Two Voices

Nonfiction
Cannibal in the Mirror
Dateline: Troy
Copier Creations
Townsend's Warbler

cannibal in the mirror

PAUL FLEISCHMAN

PHOTOGRAPHY BY JOHN WHALEN

Twenty-First Century Books
Brookfield, Connecticut

For Bob Ruddick and Gerry Greer
—Paul Fleischman

To the memory of my mother, Helen Kelley Whalen (1929–1994), who taught me how to
see the world. Her steadfast encouragement, devotion, and faith are still inspirational. I
forever owe her my deepest gratitude, respect, and love.
—John Whalen

In the interest of clarity, spelling and punctuation have been modernized.

All possible care has been taken to trace the ownership of every selection
included and to make full acknowledgment for its use. If any errors have accidentally
occurred, they will be corrected in subsequent editions, provided notification
is sent to the publishers.

Published by Twenty-First Century Books
A Division of The Millbrook Press, Inc.
2 Old New Milford Road
Brookfield, CT 06804

All photographs by John Whalen with the exception
of the following: © Michael Newman/PhotoEdit: p. 20;
© Maggie Angus, UP/GF: p. 31; © 1982 Mark Richards: p. 39;
© Corbis/Mitch Gerber: p. 40; Hulton Getty/Liaison Agency: p. 63

Library of Congress Cataloging-in-Publication Data
Cannibal in the mirror / [edited by] Paul Fleischman; photographs by John Whalen.
p.   cm.
Summary: Selections from anthropological writings are paired with photographs
of twentieth-century people engaged in similar activities.
ISBN 0-7613-0968-3 (lib. bdg.)
1. Cultural relativism—Quotations—Juvenile literature. 2. Ethnology—Quotations—Juvenile literature.
3. Primitive societies—Quotations—Juvenile literature. [1. Cultural relativism. 2. Ethnology—
Quotations. 3. Primitive societies—Quotations.]
I. Fleischman, Paul. II. Whalen, John, 1960–   .
GN345.5.C36   1999   306—dc21   98-38118   CIP AC

contents

introduction

We flip through the old *National Geographic* and smirk at the photographs of the natives. They are savages. We are modern, light-years away from them. Or are we?

"A man is known least to himself," wrote the Roman statesman Cicero. Immersed in our culture, we see its new-and-improved surface but rarely reflect on the substance below that links us to all of humankind. The microwave and the open fire both serve the same end. The family listening to an elder declaim and the family watching a movie on the VCR both have the same need for stories that entertain and instruct.

The quotations gathered here—from explorers, missionaries, and writers of many sorts—were meant by their authors to be windows on "primitive" cultures. Paired with present-day photographs, they become instead mirrors of our own customs. Turning the anthropological eye upon ourselves, looking beneath the Lycra and Formica, we're struck by how much we have in common with people of every age and place—even those often scorned as barbarous savages.

YOUTH

A heathen boy's education consists in being taught to aim skillfully with the bow, to throw the spear faultlessly at a mark, to wield powerfully the club and tomahawk, and to shoot well with musket and revolver when these can be obtained. He accompanies his father and brothers in all the wars and preparations for war, and is diligently initiated into all their cruelties and lusts, as the very prerequisite of his being regarded and acknowledged to be a man and a warrior.

Rev. James Paton, *The Story of John G. Paton Told for Young Folks, or Thirty Years Among South Sea Cannibals*, 1898

Video mall,
La Jolla, California

Cheerleaders
Palo Alto, California

youth

Ball-playing is [the Choctaws'] chief and most favorite game. . . . To move the deity to enable them to conquer the party they are to play against, they mortify themselves in a surprising manner: except a small intermission, their female relations dance out of doors all the preceding night, chanting religious notes with their shrill voices, to move Yo He Wah to be favorable to their kindred party.

James Adair, *History of the American Indians, Particularly Those Nations Adjoining to the Mississippi, East and West Florida, Georgia, South and North Carolina and Virginia*, 1775

youth

These [boys' initiation] rites occur in much the same forms in Africa, in South America, and in Australia. In South Africa the boys are herded under men with long sticks who use them freely on all occasions. They must run the gauntlet with blows raining upon them, they must expect constant blows from behind accompanied by jeers. . . . At the first signs of daybreak they must go to the pool and stay submerged in the cold water till the sun appears. They may not drink a drop of water for the three months of the initiation camp; they are fed with disgusting food.

Ruth Benedict, *Patterns of Culture*, 1934

Fraternity hazing
Storrs, Connecticut

International Debutante Ball,
New York, New York

courtship and marriage

The Australian girl is ritually "made" into a woman through ceremonies accompanied by body decoration and special hairstyles. . . . After a period of seclusion, she is bathed and makes a public entry into the main camp, accompanied by other women singing ceremonial songs. She is richly decorated, and acclaimed by members of the community as an adult woman. On Melville Island, off Darwin, the girl is painted red and yellow by the father, who also dresses her hair, building it up into a mop by twisting the curled strands of human hair on top of a bamboo chaplet, attached to which is an ornament of flattened dogs' tails set in beeswax.

• • •

Robert Brain, *The Decorated Body*, 1979

courtship and marriage

Frequently [a Moslem man] engages the services of a woman marriage broker, who has access to harems where there are marriageable women, and is employed by them quite as often as by the men. She receives fees from one party, and frequently from both. . . . If the young man is satisfied with the report of the broker, he sends her again to the harem to state his own prospects in life.

• • •

F. M. Lupton, *The Popular Cyclopedia of Useful Knowledge*, 1888

Video dating service,
Miami, Florida

Wedding cake,
Long Beach, California

courtship and marriage

Besides marriage rites which are intended to expel evil spirits or other evil influences, there are rites that are intended to safeguard bride or bridegroom by deception. . . . A traveler in Java noticed two painted wooden figures, one of a man and the other of a woman, standing at the foot of the "family nuptial couch." These figures had been placed there to cheat the devil, who, according to the belief of the people, during the wedding night hovers round the bed with a view to carrying off one of the happy pair; for it was thought that he, deceived by their resemblance, would carry off the figures instead of the sleeping lovers.

• • •

Edward Westermarck, *The History of Human Marriage*, 1921

family and society

During the dances and ceremonies in Arnhem Land, Australia, the designs painted on the participants demonstrate their membership of a particular kinship or language group. . . . Many of the blood feuds of the past were the result of a mark of disrespect towards a clan's designs or the theft of a pattern.

• • •

Robert Brain, *The Decorated Body*, 1979

Tag and cross-out,
San Diego, California

Mantelpiece and family photographs, Woodstock, Vermont

family and society

The ancestral tablet representing one's father or mother is usually worshipped only for three or five generations. During this period it is preserved with care in a portable niche, or shrine, made in the general shape of a house, but only a few feet square. If unable to procure such a niche, the tablets are simply arranged on a shelf or table.

• • •

Rev. Justus Doolittle, *Social Life of the Chinese*, 1867

family and society

W ar is the breath of their nostrils. Against most of the neighboring tribes they cherish a rancorous hatred, transmitted from father to son, and inflamed by constant aggression and retaliation. Many times a year, in every village, the Great Spirit is called upon, fasts are made, the war-parade is celebrated, and the warriors go out by handfuls at a time against the enemy.

• • •

Francis Parkman, *The Oregon Trail*, 1849

Varsity Football Team,
San Francisco, CA

CINDY'S KITCHEN

JACKIE'S KITCHEN

SHEILA'S KITCHEN

AIDA'S KITCHEN

MAGGIE'S KITCHEN

CAROL'S KITCHEN

**Gift shop,
Old Saybrook, Connecticut**

family and society

When [the Tartars] have pitched their houses with the door facing south, they arrange the master's couch at the northern end. The women's place is always on the east side. . . . The mistress of the house places on her right side, at the foot of the couch, in a prominent position, a goat-skin stuffed with wool or other material, and next to it a tiny image turned towards her attendants and the women. By the entrance on the women's side is still another idol with a cow's udder for the women who milk the cows, for this is the women's job.

• • •

William of Rubruck, *The Journey of William of Rubruck*, 13th century

family and society

To the stem of the canoe, just above the water-line, is sometimes attached a small misshapen wooden figure, which is the little tutelar deity that sees the hidden rock, and gives warning of an approaching foe. . . . Probably the Chinese custom of painting eyes on the sides of the bows of the junks, and the similar practice of the Maltese, in the case of their boats, may date back to the little gods of wood that were attached to the bows and stems of the canoes of their barbarous predecessors. The origin of the figureheads of our ships may perhaps be traced back to times of savagery when a similar superstitious practice prevailed.

• • •

H. B. Guppy, *The Solomon Islands and Their Natives*, 1887

Car Dealership,
Darien, Connecticut

Coffee break
Amarillo, Texas

recreation

All the mountain Indians are addicted more or less to the practice of masticating coca. Each man consumes, on the average, between an ounce and an ounce and a half per day, and on festival days about double that quantity. The owners of mines and plantations allow their laborers to suspend their work three times a day for the *chacchar*, which usually occupies upwards of a quarter of an hour.

• • •

Johanne Jakob von Tschudi, *Travels in Peru*, 1847

recreation

As a ritual, a test of courage and a sheer spectacle, the "land diving" performed by the villagers of Bunlap (in the Pacific island of Pentecost) is without parallel. . . . When a man is ready to jump he separates from the dancers. He climbs the tower to his platform. Two assistants wait for him. They bring up the lower end of the lianas attached to the platform. These are securely tied around the jumper's ankles. He then walks out to the end of his platform. . . . He then plunges head first toward the ground. Just as his head approaches the softened ground the lianas snap tight and the platform supports break as the tower leans forward slightly. All of this helps to absorb the shock. If the length of the vines has been correctly calculated his head just brushes the soil before rebounding in a graceful arc.

• • •

Kal Muller, *Peoples of the Earth, Vol. 1: Australia and Melanesia*, 1973

Bungee jumper,
Issaquah, Washington

Pie-eating contest,
Half Moon Bay, California

recreation

Some of [the Hurons'] feasts were on a scale of extravagant profusion. . . . In some cases, the imagined efficacy of the feast was proportioned to the rapidity with which the viands were despatched. Prizes of tobacco were offered to the most rapid feeder and the spectacle then became truly porcine.

. . .

Francis Parkman, *The Jesuits in North America*, 1867

recreation

With the returning day commenced the same round of insult and irritation. . . . It is impossible for me to describe the behavior of a people who study mischief as a science and exult in the miseries and misfortunes of their fellow-creatures.

• • •

Mungo Park, *Travels in the Interior of Africa*, 1799

Female mud-wrestling,
San Jose, California

Teenagers,
New York, New York

appearance

I kept wondering how some of [my wife's] sheltered young friends back home would act, if they were to be set down, as she was, on a sandy beach, miles from civilization, and surrounded with fierce cannibals—hideous and worse than naked; for they worship sex, and what clothing they wear calls attention to their sex rather than conceals it.

. . .

Martin Johnson, *Cannibal-Land, Adventures with a Camera in the New Hebrides*, 1922

The Aryans wear black shields, their bodies are painted black, they choose dark nights for engaging in battle; and by the very awe and ghastly hue of their army, strike the enemy with dread.

. . . .

Tacitus, *Germania*, 1st century A.D.

Skinheads,
Seattle, Washington

Autumn Fair,
Santa Fe, New Mexico

The parts of the human body which require magic protection are the orifices. Like any other openings, human orifices invite entry by demons or evil spirits. In Arab countries the eyes, especially in young children, are encrusted with magic-protective kohl on upper and lower lids. Most primitives protect the nostrils with bone, stone or metal ornaments, and Hindu ladies of wealth wear jewelled nose-rings on both nostrils, and sometimes a third between the other two. Ear entrances are universally protected by ear-rings fastened to the lobes of the ears and sometimes an ear-jewel spiralling round the ear itself. The mouth is often safeguarded by tattooing.

· · · ·

Pearl Binder, *Magic Symbols of the World*, 1972

The shape of the natural head of man particularly did not satisfy the aesthetic ideals of some North American Indians. So they laid out the infant on a flat board, giving it a pillow of moss and rabbit skins; a light plank of wood was placed at an angle so as to press upon the baby's forehead; by tying strings from the plank to the board, a continual gentle pressure was brought to bear upon the infantile skull, which was thus persuaded to grow into a peculiar towering ridge of the most extraordinary appearance.

• • •

G. F. Elliot, *The Romance of Savage Life*, 1908

AFTER A NEW LOOK?

Get the nose you've always dreamed of

- Fellow American College of Surgeons
- Board Certified
- ...than 15 years prac...
- ...ounty
- ...ry Initial...

Before

San Diego's most trusted cosmetic surgeons. We invite you to explore your options by visiting our office for a complimentary consultation. ███████ many areas of surgical expertise include **breast enhancement**, *"the natural facelift,"* fat removal through *tumescent liposuction*, nose beautification, eyelid rejuvenation, lip ...gmentation, and laser resur...

Now You Have NU⟳ OPTIONS
for Financing Cosmetic Surgery.
Key Benefits of the NuOptions Loan Progra...

Avoids the need to tie up yo...
valuable bank card lines of
credit.

Provides you with a convenie...
ow cost payment plan.

ets you enjoy the benefits o...

"WEEKEND ALTERNATIVE TO THE FACELIFT™"
with chin augmentation.

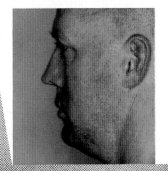
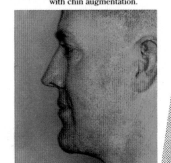

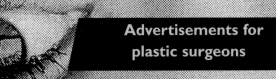

God Bless Our Home

Private home,
Chestnut Hill, Pennsylvania

beliefs

Climbing up a crude ladderway we stood on the threshold of a great arched porch that rose fifty feet above us. From the apex dangled a weird collection of amulets carved from wood. Human effigies, small crocodiles, lizards and other symbolic objects, which were to protect the house against the evil spirits of which they live in eternal dread.

. . .

beliefs

E very year these Christian, Saracen and Cathayan astrologers . . . write down the
results of their examination in certain little pamphlets for the year, which are called
Tacuin, and these are sold for a groat to all who desire to know what is coming.

• • •

Marco Polo, *The Travels of Marco Polo*, late 13th century

Newsstand, New Year's Day,
Pasadena, California

California Color Guard,
New York, New York

beliefs

Some of the tribes on our extreme northern frontier are said to believe that the whole tribe is the miraculous result of the intercourse of some god or spirit with some animal, bird, fish, or reptile. . . . The representation of that animal, bird, or reptile becomes the "coat of arms" of the whole family. Its skin, carefully stuffed, bedecked with ornaments and feathers, is tied to a staff and carried about in the hand on grand full-dress occasions.

• • •

Richard Irving Dodge, *Our Wild Indians: Thirty-three Years' Personal Experience Among the Red Men of the Great West*, 1882

beliefs

Children are carried sometimes upon the hip, but more frequently on the back, supported by the nurse's lamba being tightly fastened round her waist. The grown-up young people occasionally present a piece of money to their mothers, called fofon'damosina, i.e. "fragrance of the back," as a grateful remembrance of the time when they were carefully nursed and carried in the folds of their parents' lamba.

· · ·

James Sibree, *Madagascar and Its People*, 1870

Mother's Day card selection,
Chicago, Illinois

Montoursville baseball team,
Montoursville, Pennsylvania

beliefs

We have seen that the Melanesian mana, which is a combination of a man's character, ability, influence and power combined, can be transferred by the laying-on of hands. . . . Strength, courage, swiftness and the like can be transmitted by contact with those possessing them, or by assimilating separable parts of such persons. Hence, as is at last becoming well known, the origin and chief meaning of cannibalism.

• • •

Ernest Crawley, *The Mystic Rose: A Study of Primitive Marriage and of Primitive Thought in Its Bearing on Marriage*, 1902

old age and death

The Solomon Islanders are described as "a community where no respect whatever is shown by youth to age." Holub mentions a great cliff from which some South African tribes cast the old when tired of caring for them. Hottentots used to put decrepit old people on pack oxen and take them out into the desert, where they were left in a little hut prepared for the purpose with a little food.

• • •

William Graham Sumner, *Folkways*, 1907

Home for the aged,
Lubbock, Texas

Seven Gun Volley, Arlington
National Cemetary,
Arlington, Virginia

As soon as a death occurs the wailing begins, and at once, or possibly at sunset, the temple of the local god is visited to make the announcement to him, accompanied with more wailing. . . . Excruciating music rends the air from morn till eve, and bombs are detonating at frequent intervals to terrify malignant spirits.

• • • •

Arthur H. Smith, *Village Life in China*, 1899

When the scaffolds on which the bodies rest decay and fall to the ground, the nearest relations bury the rest of the bones, take the skulls, which are perfectly bleached and purified, and place them in circles of a hundred or more on the prairie. ... There is scarcely an hour on a pleasant day when some of these women may not be seen sitting or lying by the skull of their child or husband—talking to it in the most pleasant and endearing language they can use and seemingly getting an answer back.

•   •   •

George Catlin, *Letters and Notes on the Manners, Customs, and Condition of the North American Indians*, 1841

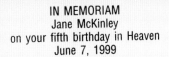

IN MEMORIAM
Jane McKinley
on your fifth birthday in Heaven
June 7, 1999

It seems like only yesterday you were here,
But for five years now, I've wandered alone.
All those years ago, I never imagined I'd be traveling this road without you.
And finally, I'm doing fine.
But still, I can't wait to see you again,
When we meet once more in Heaven.

With all the love in my heart,
Your husband, Jim

In Loving Memory Of
Maxine Q. Brindle
Two years have passed since you were taken from us. Not a day passes without us hearing your voice and seeing your smile. You are with us always. – *Your loving family*

In Memoriam
Jonah "Bud" Jones
The flowers are blooming on the hills now. How you would love the sight. It's not the same, seeing them without you. Please know that you will bloom forever in our hearts.
– *Your Children & Grandchildren*

IN MEMORIAM

In Loving Memory of
Marjorie Ann Miller
April 12, 1936 — June 9, 1996

For sixty years you gave so much
To everyone you knew;
There never was one more generous
And deeply loved than you.
For sixty years the truest friend,
Devoted mom and loving wife;
And so, instead of mourning you,
We celebrate your life.

Your loving husband, Roy,
and your children,
Alistair, Nicole and Meg

IN MEMORIAM

In Loving Memory of
Marjorie Ann Miller
April 12, 1936 — June 9, 1996

Gram, we miss you very much.
We think about you every day.
We have such happy memories of
The time before you went away.
We know you're not so far away,
You're in the rivers, trees and air.
And whenever we think of you,
We always find you there.

With love,
Julia, Sara Jean, Alex, Rebecca and Nick

IN MEMORIAM

Steven Andrews
June 10, 1953 — August 12, 1998

Not a day goes by that I don't think of you.
The sadness retreats, slowly, leaving me with only memories.
I can still see your smile, hear your voice, feel your hand in mine.
You don't seem so far away, as long as you're in my heart.

Love,
Laura

In Memoriam messages

bibliography

Adair, James. *History of the American Indians, Particularly Those Nations Adjoining to the Mississippi, East and West Florida, Georgia, South and North Carolina and Virginia*. London: E. & C. Dilly, 1775.

Benedict, Ruth. *Patterns of Culture*. New York: Houghton Mifflin Company, 1934.

Binder, Pearl. *Magic Symbols of the World*. London: Reed Consumer Books, 1972.

Brain, Robert. *The Decorated Body*. New York: HarperCollins Publishers, 1979.

Catlin, George. *Letters and Notes on the Manners, Customs, and Condition of the North American Indians*. London: Published by the Author, 1841.

Crawley, Ernest. *The Mystic Rose: A Study of Primitive Marriage and of Primitive Thought in Its Bearing on Marriage*. New York: Meridian Books, 1902.

Dodge, Richard Irving. *Our Wild Indians: Thirty-three Years' Personal Experience Among the Red Men of the Great West*. Hartford: A.D. Worthington & Co., 1882.

Doolittle, Rev. Justus. *Social Life of the Chinese*. New York: Harper & Brothers Publishers, 1867.

Elliott, G.F. *The Romance of Savage Life*. Philadelphia: J.B. Lippincott & Co., 1908.

Guppy, H.B. *The Solomon Islands and Their Natives*. London: Swan Sonnenschein, Lowrey and Company, 1887.

Hurley, Frank. *Pearls and Savages: Adventures in the Air, on Land and Sea in New Guinea*. New York: G.P. Putnam & Sons, 1924.

Johnson, Martin. *Cannibal-Land: Adventures with a Camera in the New Hebrides*. Boston: Houghton Mifflin Company, 1922.

Lupton, F.M. *The Popular Cyclopedia of Useful Knowledge*. New York: Published by the Author, 1888.

Muller, Kal. *Peoples of the Earth, Volume 1: Australia and Melanesia*. Danbury Press, 1973.

Park, Mungo. *Travels in the Interior of Africa*. Dublin: P. Dixon Hurdy, 1799.

Parkman, Francis. *The Jesuits in North America*. Boston: Little, Brown & Co., 1867.

Parkman, Francis. *The Oregon Trail*. New York: G.P. Putnam, 1849.

Paton, Rev. James. *The Story of John G. Paton Told for Young Folks, or Thirty Years Among South Sea Cannibals*. New York: Burt, 1898.

Polo, Marco. *The Travels of Marco Polo*.

Rubruck, William of. *The Journey of William of Rubruck*.

Sibree, James. *Madagascar and Its People*. London: Religious Tract Society, 1870.

Smith, Arthur H. *Village Life in China*. London: Oliphant, Anderson & Ferrier, 1899.

Sumner, William Graham. *Folkways*. Boston: Ginn, 1907.

Tacitus, *Germania*.

von Tschudi, Johanne Jakob. *Travels in Peru*. New York: Wiley & Putnam, 1847.

Westermarck, Edward. *The History of Human Marriage*. London: Macmillan and Company, 1921.